Words from my Heart
My Words, My Style
David J. Liebeg

Copyright © 2024 by David Liebeg

All rights reserved.

No portion of this book may be reproduced in any form without written permission from the publisher or author, except as permitted by U.S. copyright law.

To Mom for encouraging me all these years.

Contents

1. My given gift — 1
2. Hope — 2
3. Love — 8
4. Hurt — 33
5. Insight — 58
6. Memories — 84
7. Out of the Box — 94
8. Story Poems — 99

Also by — 103

About the author — 104

My given gift

Through my poetry, I have expressed my deepest feelings.
I have learned that I am not the only one knowing.
For those who have read my poetry, I thank you.
You help me keep me on the straight and true.
The writings that I have read, inspired me.
You have made me realize the Lord above has given me a key.
A key to tell my side of this life story.
Some words can not be written, but poetry makes a person see.
Poetry can move you with just a few words.
Echo of feelings that are never heard.
It makes you remember times of in the past.
Reflect on a future that hasn't been cast.
Words fill your head with memories loss and love.
It helps you remember the inner strength that has been given to you by a higher power from above.

Hope

Dream Keeper

Dream keeper; please keep my dream.
Of someday to be with the one I miss.
I feel like my soul is lingering in the abyss.
I lay here dreaming of her every day.
My world is covered with gray.
My life is not the same since I lost the one and only.
I wish I wasn't so lonely.
Some people think it would be a taboo.
Dream keeper; please make my dream come true.

Storm

The rain pours outside.
The wind blows; the sky and the earth collide.
Lightning flashes and a wicked loud sound fills the air.
The land and water have a love affair.
Clouds darken the sky.
Leaves are stripped from trees and fly.
Dance of the trees.
Rain keeps the beat.
Crashing of thunder; deafening.
Hail pours, the ground can not hide from the aiming.
Swirling clouds; funnel it will allow.
Trees break at their bow.
Dust and dirt penetrating the air.
Destroying everything it doesn't care.
Animals on the hoof.
Houses left without their roofs.
The wind dies down. Calm reclaims.
Life does remain.

This Day has a New Dawn

A cloud floats across the sky.
Birds begin to fly. More clouds move in.
Gray in color, rain is held within.
The wind is blowing stronger.
I should move in, I can't stay here any longer.
There are no places to hide.
No one is here to be my guide.
Rain hits my face.
With a hard steady pace.
Far off in the distance, thunder rolls from lightning that I can see.
Skies set a dark palette.
Painted by my feeling of a lonely ballot.
I want to run somewhere.
Where?, I don't care.
My tears try to hide in the rain.
Lightning goes across the sky, like links of a chain.
Dread washes over me.
Where is the end? I can not see.
I cry out loud, thunder drowns out the sound.
Where am I bound?
Warm arms wrap around my shoulders.
My heart beats a little bolder.
I look to see.
A beauty looking back at me.
Rain began to cease.
Sunlight forces through the clouds increase.
Darkness has gone.
This day has a new dawn.

I know I will be Okay

To say goodbye to a part of your past.
Even if it does hurt you and make you feel overcast.
Life moves on.
You shouldn't waste it; before you know it, it will be gone.
There is a part of my life I have to say adieu.
No matter how much I will lose.
What doesn't break you, makes you stronger.
This dread I will feel no longer.
I am tired of thinking about the what-ifs.
My heart will no longer work these night shifts.
I have opened my eyes to a better day.
No more will my soul just lay.
It took a while for this rebound.
But I stand strong with both feet on the ground.
The memories will be there, I can not make them go away.
I know I will be okay.

Little Kisses

A horn sounds, and glass shatters.
Daylight fades, and life matters.
Thoughts of her fill his mind.
The clock starts to unwind.
What will she do without him?
Will she stand tall like a tree without its limbs?
He hears his heartbeat slowing, he wonders if he can still hold his own.
His life is rushing out of him into the unknown.
Memories of his past, flash by.
He can hear her cry.
"Lord, help me through this"
A tear falls, "So I can enjoy again her sweet little kisses."
Darkness falls. . . .
He can hear her calls.
"Daddy, don't go away."
"I need you here so we can play."
He opens his eyes, to catch sight of his little angel, with tears in her eyes.
He smiles, "No, Daddy will not die."

Help

A hand reaches out from the dark, searching.
Looking for some comfort and healing.
A small voice, meek and mild, whispers.
Calling out to an ear, hoping to find a listener.
Eyes, which have been born too much.
To wipe the tears from her face, with a gentle touch.
Be strong as much as you can.
You will doubt how much you can stand.
With the help of friends, you will never fall.
Some days go by as thou it was at a crawl.
The need for strength is what you need.
To help you get through all of the day's deeds.

Love

An Angel I Can Love

Angel that was sent from the heavens on high.
The angel has put wings on my soul and now I can fly.
The darkness I was once so scared of.
Now the sun has risen and shines brightly above.
I thought I was lost, not to be found by anyone.
Once bound, now I have the freedom to run.
I have someone that I can cherish all the coming years with.
My past is now all but a myth.
There is a silver lining around every cloud.
When you feel that love can never be allowed.
It does come to find you.
I do believe that God will see you through.
I have been rescued by an angel from above.
An Angel I Can Love.

I do believe in Angels

I do believe in angels, so beautiful and face a glow.
This was arranged by some higher power many years ago.
For two people to find each other even when they are many miles apart.
But yet she in very close in my heart.
I feel her love as if I can hear it in the wind.
Her smile makes my soul come alive without end.
When the time we do meet, to touch and to hold.
Love will bring us together and keep us in its fold.
This angel of mine.
Has her own hill to climb.
At the top of this hill, she has her own angel to embrace her.
I will be there for her when life's turmoil occurs.
This angel has repaired my broken heart.
She is very amazing to mend all the many parts.

His Mate

The wolf sits and raises his head and howls.
Ears scan the air; his eyes catch sight of an owl.
In the distance, he hears a reply.
He let out another cry.
He starts to run to where the sound came.
An inner feeling comes to the surface and it is not tame.
His nose smells the air and catches a scent that drives him on.
What he is seeking, he comes upon.
His mate, the one he will remain with until the end of time.
His heart now sings a song as thou wind is passing through a wind chime.
She licks his face.
The wolf and his mate are in the right place.

Perfect Mate

In trying to find that perfect mate.
That fits just right in your heart and makes you feel great.
You might overlook someone who isn't quite right.
A relationship does not come overnight.
Both seek out each other's path.
One might get lost; give comfort to that one, don't give them wrath.
To see their journey to the end.
If the love you feel is strong and deep, both must defend.
True love does not run and hide.
True love does not get washed out with the tide.
To hold a special someone in your soul.
Doesn't mean you leave your friend out in the cold.
The flames of your love only can grow higher when you both are together.
The fire will not go out in windy weather.
Understand what each one needs.
Don't lose your way in all those weeds.
Love will conquer all and will never be too late.
Then you have found your perfect mate.

Thats Me

When you have that second thought, that's me
When you are alone and feel there is something missing, that's me
When you have that dream that you just can't remember, that's me
When you look into his eyes and there is something not right, that's me
When you look around and memory stirs, that's me.
When your heart feels empty, that's me.
When your soul yearns for something more, that's me.

Bright Future

The future for me is looking bright.
I found a woman that makes me feel right.
A little while ago I didn't think I was going to last.
I found an angel that has saved me from my past.
I do love this woman she is my heart's patch.
From heaven they know it is a match.
I will treat this woman like a lady.
I do love her greatly.
The road ahead is uncertain.
But with us being together we can go through life until the last curtain
Our hearts sing out a harmony of beautiful songs.
The love that I have for her is solid and strong.

New Beat

The heart pounds with a new beat.
Waiting for that one soul to have to keep.
When at last that time has come.
Two will become one.
The life they will share.
The love that they have will go beyond compare.
I love you with all the stars in the sky.
Until I take my last breath before I die.

The Love I have for you...

The love I have for you will last through time.
The glow of my love will forever shine.
The feeling of comfort is what I'm looking for.
I find it in your soul and so much more.
I've never felt butterflies fluttering.
When I see you my knees are quivering.
To look in your eyes I see your true soul.
A place where I can feel hot, not cold.
The love we make is very passionate.
But for now, my heart aches.
I'm missing you from afar.
The wish to be with you I would wish on a star.
To hold you in my arms.
I would be so lucky I wouldn't need any charms.
To share a dance with you.
It makes the world seem so subdued.
Every day my thoughts are on you.
Love anew.

The shortest distance

The shortest distance between two hearts is love
Love can stretch any distance, from valleys down low to mountains above.
You can try to bury it, but it takes only an instant to remember.
Years can go by, but it only takes a moment to wake it from its slumber.
They say that love is blind.
It can let us see the beauty that is hidden and unrefined.
Love can move mountains and yet not strong enough to lift a finger.
Love never goes away somewhere it still lingers.
Hits you like a bolt of lightning or it sneaks inside and not really know when.
Finding love through a friend or unconditional love from your children
Love feels like your prayers have been answered.
The sight of the one you love makes you sometimes feel like a coward.
Love can make you do things that you thought you could never do before.
We all can have that feeling of love that can open the world to a new door.

An Angel and a Wolf

The wolf, covered in snow, travels down a path he follows.
Moonbeams cast a spell of dancing on shadows.
He stops to look, silence is only broken by his heartbeat.
He stares at the moon, he feels incomplete.
A flash of light.
He wants to take flight.
But something tells him everything is right.
He gazes upon a most beautiful sight.
Wings unfold and spread wide.
An angel is what was hidden inside.
Snow sparkles around her like jewels on a crown.
"I am seeking you, TheWolf that is why I came down."
His soul is filled with love and contentment.
The world is right and not so distant.
Her glow vanishes all the shadows and the moonlight seems dim.
She kneels in front of him.
A kiss.
A feeling he can't dismiss.
I was feeling strange inside.
There is a place to hide.
Now she looks into the eyes of a man.
He cries as his feelings are overran.
She picks him up, they float into the moonlit sky.
Together they will be until forever dies.

Our Love

In our lives when we find a heart like no other;
Both need to stay the course and rely on one another.
Together love, trust, and loyalty must bind them;
Never lose or forget where those come from.
Smile along with the fun and good times that happen;
When darkness settles in, be kind, do not act like an angry dragon.
In the many years of growth and new hurdles come along;
Know that the love that drew you two together, wasn't wrong.

Many Miles

The internet holds so many possibilities.
I found someone that I can love, my heart and soul both agree.
I can see across thousands of miles, the look of love on your face.
When we meet, I know I will hold you in a forever embrace.
We exchange great pictures of us and our kids.
An arrow shot from one good cupid.
Hit both of our hearts across this great distance.
Our hearts are now in a loving alliance.
The Internet brought us together.
I know this will last forever.

An Angel holds my Heart in her Hands

An angel holds my heart in her hands.
She must be an angel because I am floating high and not wanting to land.
I swear I can see wings coming from out of her back.
She has repaired my heart, every hole, and every crack.
I can see the glow from her halo, or is it the glow of love?
I give thanks to the man up above.
I was heading down a dark road.
She came along and helped me to get rid of my heavy load.
My soul has been lifted to the highest mountain.
My love flows out for her like a beautiful fountain.
I know where we both stand.
I have an angel holding my heart in her hands.

Look of Love

When a mother and father look at a newborn.
The feeling strikes as seeing lightning from a storm.
When a child sees a puppy in the pet store.
"Can we get that puppy, I will feed it and more"
When two people meet and gaze into each one's eyes.
A feeling wells up inside and love is realized.
They both hear the singing of a dove.
On all these faces is the look of love.

Love is...

Love is that glow.
As years pass it grows.
Love is that pain.
Need for the person to remain.
Love is that feeling.
When you are with that special someone snuggling.
Love is that voice.
It tells us our hearts have made their choice.
Love is coming in those years.
When you look back remember the good times and your fears.
Love is that vision.
To see the future with absolution.
Love is that moment.
Looked into those eyes and knew what love meant.
Love is that touch.
When you press lips together the world is hushed.
Love is that thought.
When a smile strikes your face an image of your soul mate is caught.
Love is that time.
When it stood still, to start it again would be a crime.
Love is that chill.
When you see your partner, it hits you like the wind blowing off a snowy hill.
Love is.....

My Angel's Eyes

Your eyes that I gaze into.
For the future, I see what felt I always knew.
In your eyes, I see the love you hold in your heart.
I see where our journey will start.
The flames of desire dance in my Angel's eyes.
Look deeper I can see your soul fly.
Truth can be seen.
I see what I have looked for, in your eyes that gleam.

My Heart Has Wings

Love fills my heart, like hot air in a balloon.
Knowing you are not alone when you are lost and hear the call of a loon.
The sky does not seem far away.
When your soul has a place to stay.
My heart flies in the heavens, dancing from cloud to cloud.
Swooping down, landing on the highest mountain, "I LOVE YOU" I shout loud.
My time searching for you now my heart sings.
Now my heart has wings.

I Love you

Looking out on the land, hills, valleys, and plains I see.
To travel through this land, love gives you this ability.
In my life, I have climbed hills and mountains.
I have sunk into valleys and have been lost in my actions.
To look up to see another wall.
Knowing I must give it my all.
I have met an angel who has taken my hand.
To help guide me through this land.
The valleys have risen.
In this dark stormy world of mine, she has become my beacon.
The light of her love has reached my soul.
I have found a diamond in a pile of coal.
The future must have been written before.
She has a face that I will adore.
One heart plus another, are the only factors.
On this stage, we will be the only actors.
To know that you will be there to see time pass until the sun goes down.
Makes me feel as silly as a clown.
My love will grow with every day it will be like new.
'I LOVE YOU"

To Behold the Beauty

To behold the beauty that you hold.
Seems more than the unspoken words I have been told.
You have trusted me to stoke our fire.
You can look to me for what you require.
The love I feel is like a summer breeze coming off the ocean.
It fills me with warmth like a magic potion.
To look into your eyes, I can see forever.
I will be with you from now until the hereafter.
No longer do you have to wonder if there is true love out there?
Just know that I do love you and I do care.
You have the key to my gate.
I have at last found my soul mate.
The wind has blown my past into the distance.
Together we will learn throughout this experience.
Take hold of my hand.
We will cross this land.
Sharing all under the blanket of the cosmos.
Until the end draws to a close.

A Slow Dance

A slow dance draws them.
Lost into each one's eyes, forgetting the mayhem.
Steal a kiss.
Their hearts are filled with bliss.
Gracefully they glide across the floor.
The song means so much more.
Not wanting to lose their embrace.
His finger slid down her face.
Music fills the air.
Out on the dance floor, but with one care.
Moving like winds blowing in off of the ocean.
Souls sing in harmony, as the choirs of heaven.
Bodies touch.
Hearts wanting so much.
A dance of two hearts is the most wonderful sight.
Silhouettes of their form go long into the night.

Love still Remains

The seed of love keeps growing.
Beyond knowing.
Reaching for bounds unknown.
Singing a beautiful tone.
Rays of the soul, cultivate the seed and help it grow.
Having you in my life; to share, to learn.
To be by your side at every turn.
I know that our love will never wither away.
Withstanding whatever comes our way.
To see you every day is to water our love.
Like a spring rain from above.
To hear, "I Love you" pass between your lips.
Keeps the blossom of love at my fingertips.
To hold you in my embrace.
It is to know this love has been graced.
The earth may become a desert.
Love will keep growing without hurt.
The skies may cease to rain.
Still, love will remain.

Take hold of a Moonbeam

Take hold of a moonbeam.
We are about to embark on an exciting dream.
To fly through the Milky Way.
Since you came along this is where my heart will stay.
Floating in space, passing stars.
We are coming up on Mars.
The red planet bears the color of my love.
A comet passes through the skies above.
The rings of Saturn glimmer in the sun.
No exploding star will ever leave us undone.
The universe may be filled with billions of stars.
The only love I seek, I can find it where you are.
Dancing around Jupiter's moons.
We don't care if it is midnight or noon.
We'll have fun traveling through our universe.
Let us turn all the laws of nature in reverse.
Time has no meaning when I am with you.
This place we have has such a glorious view.

Walk with You

Walking with you.
Our hands lock, with this love that is new.
On a trail covered with leaves.
Smiling at each other as love sews a beautiful weave.
Squirrels leaping from tree to tree.
On a branch, sings a chickadee.
I steal a kiss, and a look of love shows through.
Uttered from your lips comes "I love you."
Breeze comes from across a small meadow.
Leaves rattle like a pleased audience clapping low.
We climb a bank, A river lies cradled.
A tree lay on the shore, weathered and mangled.
We stroll down the shore.
Knowing there is nothing we want more.
Then to never reach the river's end.
We are forever lovers and friends.

You are my Angel

You are my angel.
You have helped me win my battle.
You lift me to the highest mountain.
My life has been suddenly brighten.
The beauty of your face.
Makes my heart run at a faster pace.
I wished on a star.
You came from afar.
Floating down from the sky.
With a sparkle in your eye.
Truth is spoken from your lips.
To hear you say I love you makes my heart skip.
You have wrapped your wings about me.
The world is clear now that I can see.
You have stitched love into my soul with a golden thread.
You have a halo about your head.
Without stretched hands, you will help a friend.
Follow them to the end.
Your heart has no bounds.
You lifted up from the ground.
Never shed those wings.
Because your heart and you are a beautiful thing.

True Love

True love; always finds a place to stay.
You carry it with you from day to day.
Your heart never lies.
But you seek another just to get by.
Time will find the truth.
The heart has the proof.
To ponder why one holds that burning candle.
It would be more than you can handle.
One may never again be with that one true love.
Like one hand missing its glove.
A heart and soul will never settle for come what may.
True love, knows the place to stay.

The Beauty of Thee

The beauty of thee.
Like a carnation born of a seed.
The seed awaits in the ground.
Until the clouds weep down.
The sun casts a blanket over the seed.
The seed cracks and it comes alive and breathes.
It forces its way to see the sky.
It goes forward not knowing if it will live or die.
The carnation stretched to reach the sun.
It brings beauty to a land that feels done.
It unfolds its blossom when it is ready.
The beauty of thee.

When Two Souls Touch

When two souls touch.
You can feel the love very much.
The heavens open up in the sky.
Both hearts sitting on a mountaintop on high.
No longer traveling alone.
Never again will your heart feel like a stone.
Hands together in a forever walk.
Two souls talk.
Love fills the air.
Darkness will never again dare.
You feel butterflies.
When apart; both hearts cry.
Legs get weak.
When beholding the beauty of a face; in your mind that will keep.
Touch of your skin.
You quiver within.
A passing thought brings a smile.
Knowing you now can walk the extra mile.
Feelings of spring forever fills.
Flowers bloom on the hills.
Know you will never part even when gray hair appears.
Standing together, warding off life's spears.
Love is the one of life's greatest presents.
No longer feel as though you are a peasant.
Love wraps you in its warm embrace.
When two souls now have a place.

Love Poem

I see you throughout the town.
When I do my heart jumps leaps and bounds.
When I pass by you, my knees get weak.
I get tongue-tied when I try to speak.
One day I saw you in the park.
You were sitting under a tree, listening to a lark.
I sat across the way, so you wouldn't notice me.
I took out a piece of paper to write about your beauty.
The words flowed through my arm to my pen.
I was done before I knew what had happened.
I read it then read it again, to make sure it was right.
I am too shy to let you read my writing.
My imagination went wild.
Thinking of you and what we could do, from the hot to the mild.
Your beautiful long hair danced in the wind that softly blew.
I could feel the butterflies in my stomach, and there were quite a few.
I saw you look in my way.
My heart raced, should I run or should I stay?
I pretended not to notice her.
Inside my world is a blur.
I gathered my papers and walked down the sidewalk.
I passed by her, she looked, I couldn't talk.
I step into the street, still looking at her beauty.
A horn honked, and I saw a bus come at me.
The next thing I knew, I was looking at the sky.
I could swear an angel landed by my side.
She knelt down.
My papers floated to the ground.
The poem I wrote landed next to her.
I smiled at her, "Could you read this letter?"
You sit there next to a tree.
I picture you here next to me.

I have loved you for so long.
To come up to you to tell you, I am not that strong.
Am I silly for loving you and not even knowing your name?
But I am not, with seeing you, love came.
I feel that we are meant to be together.
I thought why bother?
I wanted to let you know, I wanted to let you see.
But I feel that we are soul mates that are never meant to be.
A tear fell from her face.
"I feel the same way, I know being with you is my place."
Tears rolled from the corner of my eye.
"I love you" was the last word I uttered before I died.

You Complete Me

To behold beauty such as yours.
Brings an angel to my door.
On the outside is not where beauty lies.
It is deep within, that makes my soul's eyes cry.
As time goes by, that beauty blossoms into the most wonderful flower.
I feel as though I am sitting on a tower.
My heart beats strong for your inner beauty.
You complete me.

Hurt

He Thinks

He thinks he is the only one to go through this.
His pain and his heart are scattered like many puzzle pieces, his tears stream down, and his miss.
He feels alone; darkness falls upon his soul,
He wants it all to end, no, wait he wants her, he doesn't know his goal.
He can't look at her, is she with someone new, "Yes, Why?"
He shared all his love; she never felt it in her heart, he wants to die.
She must have felt it; marriage was talked.
He stayed; she walked.
How is love lost, who buries it, is it still there under all the hurt?
He wanders lost, confused in his inner desert.
He sees green in the far plane.
Could it be his life will go on and remain?

Bad Day

I wish I could get over this feeling of dread and despair.
I just want it all to disappear, damn I swear.
I look up to see the bottoms of my shoes.
I feel so low, I feel like I lose.
Time is crawling by like a snail.
My soul wants to wail.
Time is supposed to be a healer of pain.
As time goes by it seems I go down the same lanes.
I'm sure people are tired of hearing me complain.
I can't remember how I was before this pain.
Can anyone help out of this rut?
I feel it clear in my gut.
Why does she have a hold of me?
Like other guys, I wish I could just set her free.
I did wrong and had no chance to correct it.
I want to throw myself into the deepest pit.
I regret so much what I feel have done.
I feel overrun.
For her to love me again would give me my life back.
But whom am I fooling; I'm in the red, not the black.
This inner feeling that things will turn back in my favor.
It's a lie.
I believe in this so much I can't see the truth, why?
When she said never come back.
I should have put my heart on a rack.
No, my heart still beats for her.
You fool, let her go, my soul is fighting with my mind, it's all a blur.

My Pain

I wish my heart didn't weigh a ton.
I used to be full of life and fun.
I wish I could get her off my mind.
She's there intertwined.
I have known her only through the summer of oh three.
But she affected me so deeply and I can't break free.
There is a deeper meaning here.
When I cannot see her I can feel, she is near.
Am I going out of my mind with all this craziness?
I should be able to move on and get away from all this mess.
She has done so much for me in the time we had.
Times I think I have forgotten her but she is there again to drive me mad.
Am I losing my sense of reality?
I know I should not keep her in here, logically.
Am I wrong?
To love someone so deep and strong.
Who has the answer to this question that rings in my head?
At night I toss and turn in my big bed.
I look towards the heavens and say, "What should I do?"
Please return her to me or make her memories fade it is overdue.
I just want to return to a normal state.
Pain still hits me like a marble slate.
Time is supposed to heal this hole in my soul.
But I feel I have no more self-control.
Driving down the road I look, in every place I look to see if I see her.
I don't know what I would do, everything seems a blur.
Just get over her people say.
It is very hard to do when you try to put it into play.
She put a spell on me and it will not flee.
What was it, her drive, her laughter, the way she did love me?
I felt the most right when I was with her than any time before.
Give me some relief, someone please, as my knees hit the floor.

A Song

Sitting at home, listening to the radio.
A song comes on and it strikes a feeling that know.
Feel the love that you put into that song.
Remembering hearing it, made the love grow strong.
Now it brings out the tears from your eyes.
You tell yourself it's no big deal, that's a lie.
Your heart hurts and that is where the start of the cry.
Before, your soul was lifted to the mountain on high.
Now your soul cowards in a corner and wants to die.
Bring back the face of an angel that God graces you with her presence.
He had faith in you to be there for her in times of need without being hesitant.
Letting your feelings flow wasn't enough for her soul to float.
Now her heart is behind a wall surrounded by a moat.
No way to break through to let her see what the future could have uncovered.
You look in the window to see if any help could be discovered.
All you see is reminders of the fun you both had in the past.
Makes you smile and maybe laugh, but it does not last.
Feeling the love that would have lasted until the rivers ran dry.
Brings another tear to your eye.
You wipe it away but more join the race until dawn.
But, that fire inside, still rages on.
You feel like you have failed at the greatest present that was ever given.
Feeling helpless that you can't let her see what she needs to believe in.
You hear that the song is now over.
But still wishing you had next to you your friend and lover.

The Love I Found in You

The love I found in you.
Made my life like new.
Sharing feelings, and dreams.
My dark clouds are gone and my soul beams.
Treasuring all the little things brought me joy.
Like a child who just received a new toy.
I thanked God for this angel he sent down to me.
The love we had felt like we had our reality.
Knowing at one point, you both felt it would never end.
But it does end.
Love seeps out of her heart like blood out of a wound that didn't mend.
Not wanting to lose what it seems you just found, you do your best.
Not really knowing the reason why, your own heart just pounds in your chest.
Feeling reality falling apart into the unknown.
You grab hold of anything until your fingers are to the bone.
Knowing when you see her again, your soul will yearn for her.
You know she's not coming back, but something makes me unsure
Something deep in me is holding onto a ghost of that special love.
I feel there is a message sent from up above.
Maybe it is just wishful thinking on my part.
But I can't deny what is in my heart.
She still is a special woman to my soul.
Maybe someday that love will be back again and she'll make me whole.

Tears of a Lonely Wolf

Wandering through the woods aimlessly.
Seeking that one he has hurt shamelessly.
Hurting inside, his heart aching to find relief.
Looking around every stone, log, and under every leaf.
Knowing he will never find his mate.
He searches in vain but he knows it's too late.
She is never coming back to grace him with her love.
He looks up into the branches and catches a flight of a dove.
He lowers his head and follows a path and climbs a hill, stands on the crest.
Starts to howl but it is more like a cry, he is a lonely wolf who tried to do his best.

Truthfully

Truthfully, my heart and soul cannot agree.
They are both in the same place but yet they have a different plea.
Confused about what I really needed.
Maybe I'm not ready like a flower that has just been seeded.
Feelings for one are new and full of hope.
Feelings for the other I am still trying to cope.
I don't want to hurt anyone for whom I care for.
Wishing that there was a simple answer to what I can't ignore.
To hold out and miss a chance to be happy,
Or move on and trust in this new love, as big as a redwood tree.

Tonight, on a Friday night

Tonight, on a Friday night I should be out.
I have this feeling of dread, no doubt
I really feel like I am alone in this life.
I wish I didn't have this strife.
I can't remember any time in my being here.
I felt this way; I wish I could find a cure.
I have a future with a very beautiful woman.
I have to wait to even meet her in person.
I can't shake this feeling
I wish I could be more appealing.
It's been this way since a few months ago.
I hide it and not let it show.
I lost someone I felt very close to.
We even going to say I do.
In times like this, I am glad for the family that I have.
They give me support and more than I need, plus half.
They try to understand what I am going through.
Truly, I don't think they have a clue.
This feeling goes down deep.
I wish my heart and soul didn't want to keep.
I just have a feeling that this is not going to go away.
But I do want it to go away so as I pray.

Emptiness

There is emptiness inside of me.
I wish I could see where I should be.
I know some people hold me dear.
I should be as high as the upper atmosphere.
Still, there is emptiness inside of me.
I have people that love me and I can see.
To find an answer to this enduring question.
I must seek it deep in me for some action.
This last year took me to the highest stairs.
And found me down on the ground with a face full of tears.
I have found someone that does love me, and I do love.
But still, I feel lost in the grove in the middle of.
I have changed in many ways from what my past has shown.
I do know that I have grown.
There is a need that I cannot see.
There is emptiness inside of me.

The gift

Finding someone special to receive the gift of love from you.
Your whole heart and soul light up with a feeling you never knew.
Make sure this gift is packaged up just right.
You give this a chance with all your might.
Talk about sharing a future together.
Knowing at that time both you can fight the worst weather.
Standing strong side by side.
Feeling your souls will never divide.
Little things count the most along the way in this endeavor.
Having trust, faith, honesty, sincerity, and hope will last forever.
But the day comes.
It starts to fall apart like a floor full of breadcrumbs.
Not wanting the journey that you both are on to end.
Seeing dreams, fade into darkness becomes very hard to comprehend
Seeking the truth of why.
Not understanding the other does not want to try.
The love you shared feels strong to you and you've shown.
Knowing your love will last, while the other's love has flown.
Your soul crumbles into so many unusable flakes.
Your heart sinks and aches.
You have tried to rekindle the fire.
But there is nothing to do from here except to retire.
As you drive away you catch a glimpse of something that is adrift.
It's the gift.

What happens to Love?

What happens to love, where does it go?
Does anyone really know?
Does it just disappear?
Does it flow out from your tears?
Does it find a corner of your heart and hide there?
Is it covered up by all the hurt feelings and it doesn't want to be bare?
If the love you had could topple mountains, why am I so scared?
If everything felt right, why can't a relationship be repaired?
Was there love there at all?
Why does one person lose love and the other can still hear love's call?
How can the one that still carries that love move on?
Will that person be forever in darkness or see the break of dawn?
Will someone help me, so I can see the sunlight from the back of a dove?
What happens to love?

Missing you

I sit here missing you.
An emptiness that I can't argue.
A smile on your face.
Like a jewel in a case.
Sparkle in your eye.
I will hold until the seas are dry.
Your voice echoes in my head.
Like a lovely book you have read.
I look at your picture.
To see the woman that I admire.
Talking to you on the phone.
Make me feel not alone.
A smile crosses my face.
When a thought hits its place.
I long to hold you in my arms.
To protect you from the world's harm.
To feel your lips on mine.
Would send me higher than the Alpines.
I will wait for your return.
So we can fall in love and burn.

A Feeling

The love I found in you.
Made my life like new.
Sharing feelings, and dreams.
My dark clouds are gone and my soul light beams.
Treasuring all the little things that bring me joy.
Like a child who just received a new toy.
I thanked God for this angel he sent down to me.
The love we feel is like we have our own reality.
Knowing at one point, you both felt it would never end.
Love seeps out of her heart like blood out of a wound that didn't mend.
Not wanting to lose what you just found, you hold tight and do your best.
Not really knowing the reason why, your heart just fell from your chest.
Feeling that reality falling apart into the unknown.
You grab hold of anything until your fingers are only bone.
Knowing when you see her again, your soul will yearn for her.
You know she not coming back, but something makes me unsure.
Something deep in me is holding onto a ghost of that special love.
I feel there is a message sent from up above.
Maybe it's just wishful thinking on my part.
But I can't deny what is in my heart.
She still is a special woman to my soul.
Maybe someday that love will be back again and she'll make me whole.

The Stage

The stage is set.
I came alive when we met.
Our heart and soul became the actors.
Learning our parts on our own, the script not written by any authors.
The lights shone bright down on us, where we stood.
Knowing the audience will think this is good.
Props were a necklace, a ring, and some flowers; to set the scene right.
Hoping no one gets stage fright.
The orchestra is preparing to play the opening music.
This play will become a classic.
Cameras peer into our eyes.
To show the real feelings, and no lies.
Cut to a happy scene.
At a park, playing around, where the grass is green.
Music plays a happy tone.
You give me a lick of your ice cream cone.
A mini-series of these memories could be shown.
We learn and the love has grown.
A storm suddenly rolls in, and thunder is heard from the west.
We felt the rain, and we tried to avoid it, but it came; we did our best.
The mood is matched by somber music from the band.
It ends faster than it began.
The scene starts to fade to black.
The stage empties and you are not coming back.
Lights go out.
My heart hears an echo when it shouts.
You left me on the stage that is now bare.
The curtains close as I continue to stare.
My soul no longer has that glow of stardom.
The flowers have lost all their pedals from their blossoms.
The chain has broken into many pieces from one whole necklace.

The ring has lost its shiny face.
Tears now cover the stage.
To look for another, Do I have the strength?
Did I miss something in the script; I searched in length.
My heart and soul are lost in debt.
I wonder about the town until I can find another stage to set.

Sitting in Fear

I sit here alone in fear.
Not knowing if the future is far or near.
Wishing I had someone to hold.
Scared to venture out into the cold.
Finding a heart that wants to beat with mine.
In fear of hearing a decline.
My heart has been broken into many parts.
Not knowing when time will heal the marks.
Having a woman that does not want me.
She doesn't want to re-open her heart with my key.
Hurt and pain have been part of her life.
Not know who will leave her in the dark or will show her the light.
I know I can be that one.
But finding my way is not fun.
To slow things down to a crawl.
Just want to curl up into a ball.
Knowing I'm the one to hurt her last.
She thinks of me as part of her past.
Knowing to myself how well she fits.
Accepting the fact I need to call it quits.
To give my hand out to her again.
She will not take it, she wants her own domain.
Knowing my downfalls in this quest.
I felt I was doing my best.

Not knowing her feelings in all of this.
Knowing a great woman to whom I'll miss.
Wishing I could take back all the times I made her cry.
Never to have the one who made my soul fly.
In time healing will come for the both of us.
Reflecting on what should have been a must.
Having a chance of love that would keep me standing.
Throwing it all away on my own lack of understanding.
Seeing now what I've done to my friend.
I shouldn't be allowed to love again.
Knowing I can't hold up my end.
Think I'm one of those gentlemen.
I know my heart is full of good.
I want to show it when it's needed and not just be misunderstood.

Looking at Pictures

Looking at pictures, a moment held.
Remembering the feelings at that time was felt.
Bringing back those memories of that day.
Happiness, fun times, thoughts stir some go, some stay.
When an image stops you and makes your heart jump.
Looking at a person that gives your throat a lump.
Thoughts of the future come into play.
Wishing you didn't hurt that person and made them go away.
That fight did not have to be.
Not being blind to that it felt so right, at least to me.
No one can take the pain and make it like it has vanished.
Having feelings of guilt and being punished.
Wanting to say you're sorry, but having it fall on deaf ears.
Makes the coming days feel like years.
Just hope forgiveness comes from a heart that is broken.
I am feeling the words that should have been spoken.

Seeing each other in the mall or out on the street.
Acting like two people who never had a chance to meet.
Knowing it deeply that each one is feeling the hurt inside.
One is willing to speak, and the other wants to hide.
Looking into each other eyes, feels like a sin.
At one time that love was held within.
Each one blames the other for the fail.
Not wanting to go back to those feelings that made your soul sail.
Maybe someday it will be worth another look.
For now, it is time to close that book.

Riddled Concrete

The rain falls to the ground.
I walk the sidewalks of this lonely town.
I catch a reflection of you in a shop window.
I turn only to see a shadow.
I look down the street.
A flashing red light, like a warning sign that I should heed.
My ear takes note of a passing sad song.
My heart remembers the lyrics and sings along.
Rain pours down on me.
My feet scuffle across this crack-riddled concrete.
I want to move out of this town.
But I feel bound.
I built this town from the love I have for you.
Now I am lost on these streets and avenues.
One by one the street lights lose their glow.
In this town, I used to know.
I spot the place where we had our first date.
We had a fun time even though the food was late.
Now the booth is empty.
Only echoes of you and me I see.

There are no cars on this street.
There is nothing for me here to keep.
I never seen any of the warning signs.
I kept between the lines.
You found your way out of this city.
Now I am the only one keeping this place from being empty.

Phone Rings

Phone rings.
I was in the middle of doing other things.
"Hello?" "It's me, please don't go" Her voice was on the other end.
Memories come flooding in.
"You are the one who didn't want to see me again." with a cracking voice.
"I know, I was wrong. I made a bad choice."
Thinking back to the last argument we had.
We both were very mad.
"Do you...umm still have feelings for me?" a timid voice came over the line.
Feelings stir in my heart and thoughts fill my mind.
I do still love her.
But do I want my life to always be a blur?
Sniffles I hear over the phone.
These feelings I have for her go all the way to the bone.
"I'd like an answer, please."
What do I say to this new lease. . . . .
"No. Good-bye."
I find my way to a corner and cry.

Outcast

On the outside looking in.
Like writing a letter without a pen.
I have a lot to say, no one to hear.
The world to me is not clear.
Can anyone understand me?
For what I can not see.
I am lost among the crowd.
I have tears, but I can't cry out loud.
I am sure that I am unsure.
"Doctor, I need a cure."
Do you know who I am? I
am the one alone, like a lost lamb.
Knock come to the door.
I open it up to see forever more.
I need to be loved and understood.
Would you be if you could?
In my own race, I come in first and last.
Outcast.

In need of a Cure

I am in need of a cure.
It will never be at the bottom of a mug of beer.
This loneliness is all about.
Turn the light on so I can see the way out.
Without you, I feel weak.
I am filled with strength when you speak.
Thoughts of you and the last time we were together.
Haunts me, like the shadows cast in gloomy weather.
I never thought I could miss someone so.
Funny, how strong love can grab your heart and soul.
When you are with that person it doesn't cross your mind.
Being apart allows sight to the blind.
I cherish the thought of us being together again.
Until such a day comes my love for you will remain.

Wedding Day

Standing in front of church doors.
I know the woman inside, for whom I adore.
By the curb is a car decorated with writing and cans on strings.
I can not help but feel what this day is and how it is a wonderful thing.
People dressed in their Sunday best.
Men dressed in tails and vests.
Women adorned by colors matching.
All to celebrate the union of two people under our Lord and King.
This day has been a long time coming.
The love I feel for this woman runs deep, it is overflowing.
I have dreamt of this day.
Know this is where my love will stay.
I walk in, music is playing, At the head of the pews, I see the most beautiful sight.
To her, this day feels so right.
I am so nervous and my knees are weak.
The preacher begins to speak.
Tears flow from women's eyes.
Far in the back, a little baby cries.
The preacher talks to the congregation, and silence, the sound of a pin drop could be carried.
"Does anyone have just cause that these two people should not be married."
My mouth remains quiet, but my heart wants to shout.
You see I am not the man on the inside looking out.
I am not the man to place that ring on her finger.
I am that man that has that love that lingers.

Was this love never meant to be?

Am I trying to right a wrong?
I am singing different lyrics to a song.
My soul is haunting the halls of my memories.
My heart bleeds for one until it empties.
Am I just making excuses not to move on?
Wandering in forever darkness, looking for the new light of dawn.
I know I should find someone new.
But feelings of old still brew.
Lord from above,
Why did you show me this love?
Then to take that love away from me.
Was this love never meant to be?
I have more questions than answers.
I feel I am lost out at sea without an anchor.
I can see land, far off, in many directions.
But are they a part of my imagination?
Why has time seemed to have stopped for me?
I feel I can not wind this clock, for I have lost the key.
There are moments when I feel that I am winning this battle.
I think I have a good foothold, but I'd fall back into all this hassle.
I look for things to keep my mind occupied.
But it seems that I am trying to cover a lie.
If there is one person for everyone on earth.
I have met her and all she is worth.
She has her own life, and she is in a fight for it.
She can see the end of the candle that is lit.
I don't know if there is anything more I can do for her.
Just to add to her mind that is probably running in a blur.
Am I worried to hear the word "No" to be spoken?
That would leave me devastated and broken.
I don't call her to ask how she is doing.
She probably thinks that I am unknowing.

I do know, but never been there myself.
To know what it feels like, not even from a book off of the shelf.
But at last, she is there and I am here.
I am chasing a dream that is not clear.
To be more honest, I can not.
This is what I go through a lot.
To hold you close to me again, my life again will begin.
People talk.
They say I should just turn and walk.
If I could I would, but what is it that keeps me here?
Wanting to hold you near.
I drive myself crazy sometimes.
Like having an open sore and applying a lime.
To watch other couples hold hands.
Leave me alone in this land.
Lord, this gift of poetry you have given me.
Help me write my feelings and be free.
But this power of the written word pales to what I am feeling inside.
I want to find a dark corner and hide.
What is this feeling that I have deep in me?
Am I afraid that I may have to wrestle for the rest of my life with this adversary?
To be proven wrong about the feelings that I am feeling now.
Too scared of letting any other feeling be allowed.

The Meeting

As I walk down the sidewalk, with my head down.
My ear picks up a familiar sound.
I look forward to seeing you across the street.
My heart skips a beat.
Before I knew it, I was next to you.
I was lost in her beauty surrounded by the sky of blue.
"Hi"

"Hi", with a meek reply. "How are you?"
Her voice sounded nervous, "all right, nothing new."
I could feel my heart pound in my chest.
She looked good the way she was dressed.
Just like the way I saw her last.
She is the one who got away in my past.
As we talked, both of us never looked each other in the eyes.
Never wanting to see the lies. We talked for a little while out in the hot sun.
Remembering when we laughed and had fun.
Feelings were rushing back.
I looked down at a crack.
"Well, I will see you around."
Where you bound?"
"No where special, Bye"
My legs felt heavy as I turned, and I let out a sigh.
Not want to go, but it is for the best.
My heart felt like a stone in my chest.
A single tear ran down my face.
Next to her is no longer my place.
I turned my head to look at her.
She was gone as though the meeting never occurred.

Wolf's Travels

The moon looms full in the sky.
The wolf glances at the moon, trying to get by.
The moon shimmers bright off his coat of fur.
He follows a trail, not knowing it might lead, thinking of her.
Through the last year, he has traveled alone.
Seeking a place where his heart can call home.
Many trails have disappeared under his feet, this year.
Yet, nothing seems to be able to hide his tears.
He lets a howl out, but nothing in return.

Wishing he could take in the lesson he has learned.
Try as he might, nothing he has done prepared him for the next day.
The trail has gone cold, but the feelings have stayed.
The loyalty has never been broken.
It stays strong through all the harsh words that have been spoken.
He has caught sight of her in his travels.
Every time his feelings come unraveled.
Tries to speak words to her. But his mind becomes a blur.
He finds a crest and howls at the full moon.
Knowing that the thought of her will still be there with every passing noon.

Prayer

Lord, do you see me?
Is there any word that can set me free?
There are times when I have everything.
Still, I have nothing.
So why am I here?
The answer is never clear.
Is it to make me think I am never right?
Or is it for me to figure out my own fight?
Do you have any clue what I go through?
Do you have direction on what I should do?
Do you have any time for me?
Or should I let things be?
I wish I had shown my heart.
But.....Where am I to start?
Have I found any solid ground?
The madness in my head is very loud.
Is there any way to let me see?
If there isn't set me free.

Silent

Silent cry.
Silent die.
Lost Love.
Thinking of.
Missing one.
No fun.
My mistake.
Cannot retake.
Still worry.
So sorry.

Insight

Bridge

No bridge's been burned that can't be mended.
Just have to come together, and grab the hand that's extended.
Mistakes will be made, but life can go on.
Just have faith and believe in the other person.
Failing to see the future and the finished task.
The bridge will fall apart and it won't last.
Working together only makes the bridge stronger.
When one falls behind, one just needs to work a little harder and longer.
Share your dreams and feelings of greater times ahead.
When crossing that bridge, not one in front of the other, but side by side instead.

After the coming of the new year

After the coming of the new year.
Life for me will be full of hills, valleys, and nowhere to steer.
This last year was filled with joy and many good times.
I have learned the meaning of love that measures many lifetimes.
I have lost loved ones through death and through a broken heart.
To look into the future and wonder if I will find my counterpart.
Memories from my recent history.
Will guide me through this new mystery.
I will never forget a few special people in which our paths have crossed.
The love that I have will never be lost.
I will hold myself to my own beliefs.
No one will steal them like a thief.
I will travel down many roads
Times that haven't come along will be full of light and heavy loads.
In this new year of two thousand and four.
I know this year will never be a bore.

Every day I battle unseen giants

Every day I battle unseen giants.
I am living my life with endless defiance.
My body feels like it's not always in my control.
But I am not going to let it defeat my soul.
Knowing if I move wrong I may not walk again.
I will not stop because of the pain.
When I am alone I'll be scared.
I won't say I am, but I don't want anyone to think I am impaired.
I will not let these giants defeat me.
I'll die of stubbornness that is my decree.

Forgiveness

Forgiveness is looking beyond.
Forgiveness is not letting evil respond.
Forgiveness is having the heart to say I understand.
Forgiveness is hard feelings that don't have any place to be grand.
Forgiveness is seeking the truth from your soul.
Forgiveness is not acting angry, and cold like a troll.
Forgiveness is feeling enlightened that your soul has no debts.
Forgiveness is not having any regrets
Forgiveness is finding the strength from up above.
Forgiveness is having the gift of love.

A few words to draw a picture

It only takes a few words to draw a picture.
You don't need to come up with a lecture.
Feelings in your heart and soul are all you need.
Start writing and let your heart take the lead.
Feelings of happiness, sadness, anger, and all others can be the subject.
Don't be afraid that your writing will be a reject.
There is someone out there who can relate.
Just let it come out through the gate.
When it comes from down deep inside.
You will never be left on the outside.
This is my guarantee of yours and my rite.
When you can see a picture of what you wrote, you got it right.

When a person that you do love, passes

When a person that you do love, passes away so suddenly.
Cherish the memories that you had together, and pray for their new journey.
Take time to reflect on the past, remember the good times, and smile.
That person chooses you to be with for a long while.
The love they gave, will carry you through the years.
Don't be afraid to shed some tears.
For that's where the love that you have to show.
They are in God's care, they do know you love them, they just know.

Mirror

Love and hate, there's a fine line that divides.
The amount of love you give is a mirror for hate that is applied.
The anger that comes from that love.
Hate fits like a glove.
Stand up take that mirror and throw it to the floor.
For every piece that shatters, feel the love that you had before.
Cherish those feelings, don't let that hate have the strength to rise.
You will be a better person than the others who are unwise.
Then you can see and feel yourself in a different mirror.
Love will reflect, and life will be clearer.

Children of Mine

Time seems to go flying by.
You say goodbye before you have time to say hi.
Children grow up with the guidance you offer.
Hoping that they will use that knowledge in their adventure.
To see my children learn a new subject.
They mold that idea into a new object.
Like fireflies dancing in the dark.
That glow of learning will guide them through to leave their mark.
Spending time with them, hearing what they have to say.
Makes the time seem like it wants to stay.
But time does move ahead.
You can look back and see how your children were led.
Knowing that there is no mountain they can't climb.
I am proud of these children of mine.

Peace

Why do people commit crimes?
I wish it would end in my time.
When people kill others is just not right.
Families and friends cry for many nights.
News people report what they know.
They report that there is no better tomorrow.
I just wish people could get along.
It would make this whole world strong.
Killing each other is not the way.
I want this world to be at peace and make it all go away.
Animals kill when they need to.
We should all take their view.

Our Mother

When we seek the truth, our mother is there.
When we are down, she makes us feel like a millionaire.
I dedicate this poem to my mother.
No other would ever replace her.
She is a strong woman and wise.
When times are gray, she makes the sunrise.
We are proud of her life achievements in the time she has been on earth.
Surviving us kids and the loss of the one she deeply loves.
Mom is an angel sent from the one from above.
We all love her with every part of our soul.
She is the one that makes us whole.
I know you love us with all your heart.
This family is strong and you are the major part.
Thank you for all that you have done for your children.
Let God shine down on you and let you live for a long time to come, Amen.

Nowhere to Turn

When a person doesn't know where to turn.
Look towards a friend that wants to learn.
A friend who does care to listen to you.
In the past, we talked when you felt blue.
My door is always open.
I am sorry for what happened back then.
The love that I have for you does not end.
I can help you out as a good friend.
The world does not have to seem so big.
If you feel as fragile as a twig.
I can never promise you that I can make you feel like new.
But I will listen and maybe guide you through.
You can talk to me until you are blue in the face.
Just remember you always have a friend in my place.

A Journey

Until my inner world knows its bounds
For me, there is nowhere for me to be found.
The truth of my life is a reality yet to be seen.
The life that I want to know, is for now a dream.
To all who know me, the inner truth is what I need to speak.
To the one that has witnessed my strength, I feel weak.
I wish all could know who I really am.
I am a very confused man.
I beg for those who just don't understand.
I need to change my life's plan.
To rush forth would be mute.
There is no time to play nice and cute.
My nutshell of the world has just been cracked.
I need to listen to my soul for my facts.
This journey I have already begun.
Will not end with the next setting sun.
The inner love that I need to find.
Needs to be known by the deaf and the blind.
All the wrongs I have done.
I hope in time, forgiveness will come.
Don't feel sorry for me.
Just be there with your eyes to see.
I need not to lie.
To find out just who am I.

Standing Still

When life seems to be standing still.
It is time to reflect and mill.
Over the past and what is to come in the future.
Not being sad about what was lost but finding a cure.
Learning from what went wrong.
What does not kill you will make you strong.
Life does travel on and it does not yield.
Pick yourself up and the better you will feel.
In losing a friend, look for the lessons you have to gain.
Being real to the fact that time will ease the pain.
Wishing time would somehow go back.
When you had that person, now you lack.
Knowing that the love you gave.
Will now in times of need will make you brave.
That you will live through very hard moments in time.
That you are worth more than a dime.
Open your eyes up to see the light.
To have the strength to say "Yes, I can win this fight."

Take every day like it is a new door

When that door is opened, let the past guide you.
Don't let it blind you to the fact of what the future can do.
Taking time to see how the day will end.
If you seek an answer, find it within, or confide in a friend.
The strength of that day will always help you for the next day.
Don't be afraid to take chances before they go away.
Listen to your heart and it will give you freedom.
If you come to regret your choices, then your choice, from the heart didn't come.

A strange new world

A strange new world is about to be revealed.
Afraid of letting your soul be unsealed.
You are putting the old world away in your mind.
Hoping the new one is gentler and kind.
To see that the sky is blue and the grass is green.
Stepping into the vast new scene.
Looking towards the horizon, I saw a new friend.
They will not let you down at the end.
Remaining friends with the past.
It will help you put a strong wind in your mast.
To sail into the future with strong sense of whom you are.
Makes you stronger and where you can find your own star.

A true friend I am

Life is a road you travel on.
Soon enough it will be gone.
You never know who you will come across.
Don't make friends into enemies, that would be a great loss.
In the future, you might need someone when you are in dire lands.
You look to see who could help, and no one stands.
You feel alone, knowing you shouldn't been so cold.
The weight of losing friends from your past becomes a heavy load.
Then in the far reaches of your view, a figure walks towards you.
A shallow breath you drew.
As he comes closer, tears start to flow,
I told him I never wanted to see him again and told him to go.
Memories of the past hit you like a shot.
Memories that you didn't want to resurface and thought you forgot.
Should I tell him I don't want him here?
A spark of a feeling comes from out of nowhere.
A feeling of a once raging love, all there is now is a faint ember.
When you last saw him, he was hurting as you remember back then.
Feelings start to stir from within.
Why does he want to help me I cause him so much mayhem.
He lifts your lowered head said, "A true friend I am."

Eyes

Eyes are a look into the inner soul.
You could see a diamond or a lump of coal.
To peer into someone's eyes.
Is like a look into what the soul cries.
There is a feeling that you can feel.
To look is to see what is real.
In order to see what you can not see.
The eyes are a doorway to love or a lie that you can believe.
If you really don't look into someone's eyes.
It is a feeling that you are missing and at your own demise.
To connect with that person.
Their eyes are the liaison.
Don't go on what people say.
The eyes can either say yes or nay.

Life's Journey

In life, everything happens for a reason.
When you feel that you have been abandoned.
It might take some time to see the reason why.
Have faith in what is to come, don't lay down and die.
To try to see what will happen in this adventure.
You end up not seeing the picture.
Certainties in life are not clear.
Like fighting a disease without a cure.
Time does have a way to make bad times in life, fade.
One day things will come to light, don't hide behind life's masquerade.
To fall victim to this demise.
You will never know what are truths and what are lies.
Path of life's journey, with all the hills and valleys.
Just seek deep inside of you to find all of your abilities.
Things will work out in the end.
To try to think it out, It would be very hard to comprehend.

Touch of a Heart

Touch of a heart.
Like a piece of great art.
It moves you.
Like before you never knew.
You feel the embrace.
Just with the sight of that face.
The smile.
That freed you from exile.
The loss.
For times you got a toss.
Brings tears.
For the loneliness you felt for years.
The soul that bears a mark.
Touch of a heart

Uncharted Territory

You find yourself in a strange land.
Not knowing where you are going, or even where you stand.
Everything looks unfamiliar, strange to you.
Not having a single clue.
Where this path in front of you will lead.
Forest looks dark and deep, wanting to run at your fastest speed.
But cautiously you make your way.
Because where you came from you couldn't stay.
Ahead lies an uncharted territory.
It seems to you that it is a scary story.
Wanting to skip to the end.
To find out if you will survive, but the end has not been written.
Believe in yourself to make it through.
Someday you'll know every avenue.
Trust that you have the knowledge.
You are strong enough not to fall over the edge.

Shaky Floor

As I look toward my future.
My past puts it into measure.
I look inwards to see outward.
Moving forward on this road, every now and then I look backward.
I have found my path.
Built with pain and wrath.
I need to keep it on the straight and narrow.
Really listen to the song of a newborn sparrow.
To hear the chance of a new day.
Finding my way.
I have a new sense of self.
This good luck didn't come from an elf.
I have looked towards the skies.
Opened my eyes.
To what is needed in my life to make me happy.
Like a child that worked hard for a piece of candy.
The dread I feel comes and goes.
I do have my highs and lows.
But life is full of those days.
I have found some new alleyways.
To detour my thoughts to good thoughts.
See the stars through the eyes of an astronaut.
I don't look toward the horizon anymore.
I take it step by step on this new shaky floor.

Healing

An old broken-down bridge spans a valley.
Look to the other side you see where you want to be.
Turn your head to see the long hard road you have journeyed down.
The life that you have had makes you frown.
The love that you have lost.
Is no longer worth the cost.
The bridge you see.
This leads to a better place where you will be happy.
Taking the first step is very hard.
Changing your life is not like a stroll in your backyard.
The life you knew and grew up in.
You will carry it with you and every now and then will make you grin.
Slowly stepping towards what you seek.
Soon, it will be as strong as concrete under your feet.
Reaching the other side, you have found your goal.
You can feel the healing of your heart and soul.

Fighting Fears

A sad little girl alone and in a corner.
People passing her, acting like she is a foreigner.
Tears fall to the sidewalk below.
She is lost and doesn't know where to go.
She sniffles; "Can anyone help me, I am lost?"
A coin lands at her feet from a passing man that he had tossed.
Walks down the street.
Stop to sit on a bench to rest her feet.
She feels a warm hand being placed on her hand.
She looks to see a man.
She had never seen a man with a glow.
Tears dried up as he caught the last of the flow.
"I am lost." in an unsure voice to the man.
"I'll take you home," he said taking her hand.
On the way, he hardly spoke.
She saw her mom's arms open; her face now tear-soaked.
"I am glad you are home and that you are okay."
"This man showed me the way."
"What man, hun?"
The little girl looked to where she had run.
No one was there.
"There was man with a glow, he was the only one that care."
She saw on her mother's face a smile and a single tear.
Look to heaven to help fight the fears.

Fade my Light

Fighting a fear.
Holding back the tears.
Summoning the strength to go through it.
Knowing realization has hit.
I have gone through this before.
It doesn't help trying to open that door.
Can I take any more of this?
Wish it would go away with a kiss.
I know I am strong but I feel I am getting weaker all the time.
Why was I cursed with this crime?
I seek a helping hand.
Feeling quite alone in this land.
Been so many years since I felt this way.
Hoping beyond hope that this would disappear and not stay.
I have to battle this beast and make it run.
It has arisen again and it has a bigger gun.
Courage is what I need to stand my ground.
To stand on own my two feet and not let this get me down.
When I need extra support.
I have friends and family to bring to my court.
I will win this fight.
I am too stubborn to let this fade my light.

My Life's Road

As I stand on the road of my life, my shadow stretches out long.
I look at where I came from, I remember when I was strong.
All the hills, valleys, and side roads lead me to you.
From that day forward, I became half the man all knew.
Now I travel down this road alone.
Sometimes too weak to pick up a small stone.
A fork is up ahead for me.
Should I go left or right, not sure completely.
You gave me direction, as we both ventured down this road.
Alone, I can barely carry this heavy load.
I look for a message on every billboard.
A house with an open door.
I turn my lights on at the end of the day.
Remembering you helped me not to lose my way.
I have lost more than I have gained.
My life's road will not be the same.

Why can't this forest stay?

I take a walk down a path in the woods.
I passed where a great tree once stood.
Thoughts come to mind of how long that tree grew.
What it could tell of what it knew.
It stood up to a lot of different weather.
Protecting baby birds in their nests of feathers.
It stood strong against the rain and the winds.
It supported life with every leaf on its limbs.
Now this mighty tree has fallen.
Never again to hear the bird in its branches call'n.
Nature did not take this tree down.
Man give the reason, we need more ground.
The forest grows smaller every day.
The wolf howls a cry,
Why can't this forest stay?

Star

As I travel through this darkness.
Walls of my soul are drenched in loneliness.
But I turn my head to the sky.
I see a single star that has caught my eye.
This star helps me to put a smile on my face.
It gives warmth in this cold place.
Once had shown brighter than the sun.
Now it is a reminder of a past that is all but done.
When I look upon this star, it takes me a to time that has gone by.
I used to ask, how it grew dim and why.
Realization has told me that this star will always be part of my world.
It is an anchor when my seas start to whirl.
For me, this star will always burn.
Will be there for me at every turn.
I can no longer travel to this star.
No matter how many steps I take it will still be too far.
So it will remain there for me, over my shoulder, up in the sky.
Until the time when my inner star does fade and die.

A Child's Eyes

The world through a child's eyes.
They see the truest truth, and they don't see the lies.
To them, the world is so simple and plain.
They don't think of any of the pain.
The color of skin matters not.
Children play all together until they are tied in a knot.
Children may not know everything.
Adults can learn a lot from children when they sing.
Children lose their childish ways soon enough.
Sit with a child and listen and learn when you think the world is rough.

A Tear

A single tear streams down your cheek.
It is filled with emotion both strong and weak.
To peer into this tear, you would see the pain.
Made of nothing more than water, but leaves a stain.
Reflection of someone waving goodbye.
Getting through a lie.
Fear of letting go.
Like a child hearing the word "No".
A world can be found inside of a tear.
Never knowing if the end is far or near.
A moment of time forever held.
Hearts of stone even can melt.

Snowflakes

"Why are all the snowflakes different, Daddy?"
I turned to my son, waiting for my reply so eagerly.
"Well, son, I don't know."
He looked down and wiped his runny nose.
He jumped off the park bench and stared at all the people enjoying the winter's day.
Kids throwing snow, skating, building snowmen, and even some grown-ups at play.
"Dad, I think I know the answer to my question."
"Yes?" waiting for his explanation.
"You see all these people out here today."
The dad pauses, "They are different in their own way."
He looked up at me with a small glow.
"Just like snow."
I pick my son up and sit him on my knee, as my smile grows.
Amazing what children know.
"We all are different, but when we all get along, it is a wonderful sight."
"Just like when the snow falls, Dad, right?"

Memories

God gave us his son

God gave his only son to us.
Join in the message that was brought by Jesus.
As Jesus lay in the manger, in that little stall.
He held in his heart and soul, love, and forgiveness for us all.
On Christmas day, and throughout the rest of the year.
Let us rejoice in this celebration, and let us not bring a tear.
Turn to your fellow person, and hold out a helping hand with all you are worth.
We all can live in peace on this place we call Earth.
Remember all that has touched your life.
Forgive them if they gave you any strife.
Cherish all that people can give you.
It will make your heart feel new.
Merry Christmas to all, I hope you get what you want in that package.
Just remember his message.

Happy Birthday

To: My special someone.
From: Your special someone
I am very happy you found me from afar.
If not I would never know who you are.
You have done so much for me.
You have brought more life to me than what is in the sea.
To have the chance to fall in love with you again every day.
I know, together we handle come what may.
We were brought together from the stars above.
HAPPY BIRTHDAY MY LOVE.

Christmas

As we celebrate every Christmas Day.
We see children open their presents and play.
Snap, crackle, and popping sounds are coming from the warm fireplace.
The smells coming from the kitchen puts a smile on your face
Listening to family and friends laughing and talking.
Digging for candy and other surprises in your stocking.
The memories of Christmas past.

It is Christmas Eve night

It is Christmas Eve night.
The night is long; I wish that you were here with all my might.
My heart and soul are empty
Soon the house will be full of cheer and there is plenty.
My mind wanders to a place that I want to be.
Family and friends will be here filled with glee.
Yet my lonely soul is trying to find a place of wanting.
Years have gone by through summer, fall, winter, and spring.
In times like these; I need you next to me.
I'd be so happy

On this Christmas night

All the gifts have been given with good cheer.
Everyone is sharing laughs, remembering the past year.
Children are playing with their new toys.
Thanking God for blessing you with all your girls and boys.
Snowflakes are falling outside, I stare out into the darkness.
Looking like diamonds falling from the sky, sparkling with shininess.
I should be happy with having all my family around.
Deep inside I feel alone, my soul cries without making a sound.
Wishing on that one gift that I had before.
To look into those eyes, that I loved to explore.
To feel that touch of a warm hand on mine.
That made me feel strong inside and made my face shine.
You smile at a joke that was told, but I feel empty inside.
I go for a walk, listening to the silence outside.
Hearing the snow crackling as it joins the snow on the ground.
Tears well up in your eyes and then pour down.
I miss; I hurt, wishing that I had her by my side.
It is hard for me to keep my spirits on the upside.
I look up into the sky.
Wondering if I will get by.
I search for that one special light.
But my heart and soul are having a silent night.

On this day we give thanks

On this day we give thanks for all the gifts we hold dear.
Take time to reflect on those who bring us tears.
Ones that are here and ones that we hold in our hearts.
Wishing your friend was here next to us to embrace them and not be apart.
Look around and see friends and family gathered on this day at last.
It is time to forgive all that has happened in the past.
So smile, have fun, and laugh like there is no tomorrow.
The time we have with each other is the time that we borrow.
Cherish the family and friends that are in the foreground.
Keep the ones in your soul that are not around.
Tip your heads up and look towards the heavens above.
Give thanks to the one who gave us each other and Love.

A Christmas Message

On this Christmas day, we cherish the gifts that God has given.
Family and friends gather to pray and know that they are forgiven.
As we open the gifts that are around the tree.
We reflect on the last year, knowing it is almost gone completely.
People that made us laugh and made us believe we couldn't stop.
People who help us in times of need and make us feel on top.
Take the time to forgive all who have done you wrong.
Life is too short to carry this heavy burden; it will help your soul to become strong.
That is one of God's greatest gifts that he blessed us with.
To accept forgiveness in our hearts will take us to that place that is not a myth.
Don't let any regrets or hurt feelings have a place to reside.
The love you carry for others is still deep inside.
Remember the family and friends that you have lost.
Ones that have passed, the ones who are still here, hold them dear to your heart at any cost.
Think of the ones that don't have friends or family.
Find it in yourself to bring them hope and love, that is the key.
The world doesn't need all of these harsh feelings.
If everyone finds love for his or her fellow humans, the world will start healing.
We all can believe in ourselves and others.
In the whole scheme of God's plan, we are all sisters and brothers.
Having faith the world can become a better place.
You will be placed in God's grace.

A Christmas Wish

I have a Christmas wish that comes from my heart.
I don't need to go to a mall or put in a cart.
Wishing that the one I do truly love comes back to me.
I would be filled with joy if she would be under the Christmas tree.
Losing someone so close to Christmas with whom I felt she was my soul mate.
My feelings of all twisted up inside, and it was hard to navigate.
I have friends and family that love me.
But still, I'm not filled with glee.
I wish she knew that I am sincere.
It would be the greatest gift for me it would make my smile reappear.
The only present I want to open is the package of love wrapped up inside of her heart.
But it is wrapped under many layers of hurt and mistrust; I just wish I knew how to start.
I was the one who put the final touches on that package.
I just wish she would understand my message.
If a miracle would happen on that day.
I would not let her go like wrapping paper that gets thrown away.

Mother's Day

There is a day set aside for all the mothers out there.
Ones for whom give out freely their love and care.
Ones who stayed up late at night when you were sick in bed.
One helped sort out the confusion in your head.
Ones who love you no matter what you have done.
Ones who give a helping hand out to their hurting sons.
Ones who gave comfort to their daughters when life seemed too much.
Ones who could put a smile on your face with just a touch.
Ones who worry about their children no matter what age they are.
Ones whose gray hair started when you started to drive a car.
Ones where you found shelter when a storm a brewing outside.
Ones who offer words of wisdom as a guide.
Ones who believe in you even when no one else did.
Ones who still act like a kid.
Ones who give their all to make sure their children's lives turn out right.
Ones who give you a hug and kiss before bed at night.
Ones who have the strength to overcome their own problems.
Ones who love to see their children blossom.
Ones who wipe the tears away.
Ones whom your love will always stay.
A mother is the next best person to the man above.
I don't think one day is long enough for a mother's love.

February 14th

On February 14th, we celebrate the love we hold towards one another.
We hold love for that one that is like no other.
One day set aside to to say I love you.
Love is not bound to one day, everyday love should be shown anew.
We buy red roses and gifts to show.
Love comes from the heart, not something that comes with a barcode.
To celebrate love in its truest form.
All you need is to feel another's heart that is warm.
For the ones that only show love on that day.
Love will not stay.

To Share

A day dedicated to love is Valentine's Day.
You find just the right words to say.
To express what you feel for your soulmate.
Showing your love that you still feel that special moment from your first date.
An evening out, or alone without anyone around.
A bouquet of flowers pick from out of the ground.
Recapturing that feeling that maybe has been lost throughout the last years.
To share so much on that day it brings some tears.
Enjoy each other and learn a little that you did not know.
Sit back and look at your partner to see that glow.
To feel it deep inside.
Trust that feeling to be a guide.
Hold that love and never let it go away.
Because the love you have now might be lost by next Valentine's Day.

Out of the Box

Old Wagon Wheel

An old wagon wheel sits against a rock in the west.
Back in the time when it carried people to new places to try to do their best.
Wagon it carried, full of a family's dearest possessions.
Did they make it,? or did they have to abandon their mission?
They started in the East with a dream.
This old wagon wheel, falling apart and looking very well used as it seems.
How many times did it go around?
Now half buried in the ground.
Places it has passed are no longer on a map.
Was this wheel caught in some horrible mishap?
My mind wonders about the people of old.
Should be proud of them they were adventurous and bold.

Nature

Taking a walk into the back woods.
I love seeking nature as much as I can.
Seeing birds, squirrels, and occasional deer.
I grew up learning about nature, I wouldn't like to see it disappear.
This world has been around longer than we have been here.
Nature took hold and some of us turned a deaf ear.
It is up to us to keep all animals alive and in the neighborhood.
So we all can take a walk into the backwoods.

The Snow

The snow of the winter covers up the autumn color.
Flakes fall to the ground, floating lightly down, one not like the other.
The land, trees and everything looks fresh and new.
Out in the countryside, it's so quiet as if you listening to a statue.
Fluffy snow fills your footsteps as you walk.
As the wind blows, trees begin to crack and talk.
Soon the winter will melt into spring.
You can always remember when the snow was a beautiful thing.

A Dragon's Plight

No one understands me.
They think I am terrible and ugly.
I do my best not to hurt anyone.
They either want to kill me or turn and run.
I see my reflection in a lake.
I can feel my heart ache.
Yes, I have wings and a long tail.
But these shouldn't give people a reason to wail.
My body is covered with scales, and I have a set of horns.
Yet I mourn.
I could be your best friend.
With my size, I could protect until the end.
I curl up in a corner with my wings around.
My tears fall to the ground.
I could fly to any place I wanted to.
But all I would hear are the same hisses and boo's.
So I stay here, fighting off knights and scaring the village people.
I have a fiery breath at my disposal.
it is for defense that is all.
I just wish people wouldn't get a fright.
This is a dragon's plight.

Land can be seen from my bow

Lost on this wide open sea.
Searching for something, desperately.
Dark clouds blot out the sun.
Thunder rolls across the sky, sounding like a thousand guns.
The sea is stirred up, cooking an evil brew.
I am all alone without a crew.
Water swells, and the ship rocks from side to side.
The mast strains and let out a loud cry.
Clothes drenched, fingers aching.
Trying to survive, feeling that my back is breaking.
Only seeing briefly with every streak of lightning.
Sails rip away.
Flapping on deck where they lay.
My ship thrashes from wave to wave.
I do not want a watery grave.
The helm spins wildly out of control.
As the ship banks and rolls.
A loud cry from down below is heard.
As the port side loses the battle with the rocks.
My heart pounds and knocks.
The ship is taking on water.
I fall to my knees and pray to my Savior.
"Lord, Help me through this night."
A pause, "I am filled with fear and fright."
My tears melt together with the rain.
"I can not take too much more of my pain."
A whisper carried through the air, strikes my ear.
"Have faith in me, give yourself to me and I will steer."
A ray of light filters through the dark, illuminating my soul.
My ship ceased to roll.
"Thank you, Lord"

"Take my hand, I will guide you to the door."
The seas are calm now.
Land can be seen from my bow.

Rain

As the rain falls to the ground.
It has a calming sound.
Raindrops make ripples in the water.
Never knowing where they will come down, It never matters.
Leaves in the trees, sound like they are clapping for the refreshing rain.
Water travels down the lane.
Running as far as it can go before it disappears.
The rain drips off of the angel statue in the garden like tears.
A robin is out in the yard looking for a meal.
Worms crawl away, not liking this deal.
Life is helpful along with every drop of rain.
As I think of what nature can do, I know we all can gain.

Story Poems

Wolfhaven

Off in the distance, an ominous castle stands.
The moat is murky and black.
War-torn brick walls riddled with cracks.
Trees burnt and wickedly bent.
At another time this castle looked pristine and different.
This stronghold now is home to a fierce dragon.
I am here to slay this beast and to reclaim this castle called WolfHaven.
On my horse, I cross the draw bridge.
I see the remains of past knights displayed up on a high ledge.
I travel into the depths of the large walls.
"Come out and fight me, ye old mangy beast." I call.
Back in the darkness, red glowing eyes appear.
A loud snort as the dragon's head rears.
Stepping out into the light of the courtyard, wings spread, he peers at me.
Flares his lip as he snarls and shows his teeth.
Like a silent alarm went off we both leap into battle.
Fire flies from his mouth, the heat is unbearable.
Jumping off to the side.
I throw my spear, hoping it takes a good guide.
It strikes the beast, he lets out a loud cry.
"As my name is TheWolf, today you will DIE!"
I leaped for the spear, spun, and landed on his head.

"No longer will you hold this land in dread."
The dragon tries to shake me.
Flapping his massive wing, clouds of dust and debris.
To the air he flies, I grab onto his horn.
He roared loudly like a tremendous thunderstorm.
Climbed higher and higher into the sky we went.
He spun around and headed toward the ground; hell-bent.
I pulled my sword out of the sheath.
I drove it deep into its head as I gritted my teeth.
He threw his head back.
He hit the ground with a big crack.
I fell to the ground.
The force of the plunge made a deep mound.
I sprung to my feet.
Dragon does not want to admit to his defeat.
He let out a roar, but he lost too much.
Death has got him in it's clutch.
I stand there watching him.
The light in his eyes grows dim.
With one final growl, he perishes.
The tale of TheWolf will go on for ages
I rode into town on my horse over the cobbled street.
People gather around to join in on the dragon's defeat.
Smiles and cheers fill the air.
"I have conquered the beast, where no one else would dare."
As I dismount my horse, I hear a familiar voice.
I turn to see the one I love over all the other choices.
"I feared you wouldn't come back"
"Not even the heat from the dragon's breath, would make you wear black"
I wipe a tear from her eye.
"You need not to cry."
A smile filled her face.
Our lips found their place.
The assemblage let out a grand cheer.
We move into the house away from the crowd's leer.
I pull her towards me.
To feel her close to me, made me feel complete.
Our lips met, and we kissed for what seemed like forever.
I could feel the heat of her body as I caressed the face of my lover.
I looked deep into her eyes.

I could see where my passion lies.
She guided me over to our bed.
All the past days have fled.
"I am here for you"
As my desire for her grew.
Our clothes met the floor.
To see her in this candlelight made me want her more.
I layed her back on the bed.
I softly kiss her head.
My mouth searches out hers.
The feel of her nude body against mine, I know I found the cure for my desire.
We tossed in the bed until our shadows disappeared in the dark.
Morning came, and I was wakened by the song of a lark
I turned to see a vision of an angel next to me.
Her hair tossed across the pillow, I thank the man above for this beauty I see.

Tales of TheWolf

The sound of hooves pounding the ground.
The sun starts to stretch its reach across the battleground.
Men adorned in shiny armor, swords, and spears, they are ready for this war.
TheWolf surveys his enemy, from one side to the other, he has never seen so many before.
He turns to his men and catches the warrior's soul in their eyes.
He nods, A cry of a horn fills the sky.
"Our enemy will cover the battlefield with their blood!" He yells.
The ground rumbles like demons being released from hell.
The enemy advanced, numbering in a hundred thousand.
The sound of metal clashing could be heard across the land.
TheWolf strikes his foes down one by one. Swords flashing in the sun.
TheWolf feels the sting of a sword blade that glanced at his arm.
He looks at his adversary, "I am going do you great harm."
He smiles as his sword comes around and hits its mark.

"I told you," TheWolf said as his enemy's eyes fell dark.
He turns to view the progress.
Hard to see through all this bloodshed and mess.
The enemy had taken advantage of their numbers.
But his men are courageous fighters.
The battle goes on well into the night.
Men could be heard by their calls of fright.
TheWolf lays his eyes on their leader.
"You will now meet your creator."
He pulls his sword out of a slain foe.
"Turn and face me, Avensto."
Avensto turns, face bares scars from a battle now long forgotten.
"Do you think I am scared of you and your small band of barbarians"
TheWolf raised his sword.
The blade cut the air as Avensto leaped backward.
Avensto lunges towards him, he blocks, and he glares.
The clang of the blades sends a crack through the air.
All the men stop fighting, to watch these two rivals fight.
"You will not win tonight"
"My men and I will kill you and your despicable pack from WolfHaven."
The men's silhouette could be seen against the moon that has risen.
They fought with all their strength.
TheWolf will never give up at any length.
With a hard blow, Avensto falls to the ground.
A scream was let out as TheWolf drove his sword in; then not a sound.
With blood and sweat dripping from his face.
He looks up to see everyone just standing in their place.
The enemy dropped their weapons and ran.
"Bunch of chicken. Run away this is our land."
The sun crests the hill.
The flag of WolfHaven blows in the wind and gives TheWolf a chill.

Also by

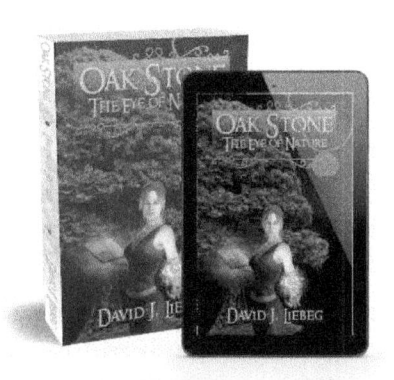

About the author

WWW.MYWORLDS.NET

I love writing fantasy books because it allows me to explore the magical world I always wanted to live in. I can create a world where anything is possible and the only limit is my imagination.

I also have written poetry. It helps me wander through the inner me, my thoughts, and emotions. I also like to have fun with it.

I hope you enjoy my books as much as I love to write them.

Thank you.